A Psalm Unto You

A Psalm Unto You

Jas Taylor

For God.

Though many may never know the intricate details, you know my story. You know *me*. You know me at my innermost, vulnerable self. You saved me spiritually, physically and emotionally. You witnessed and comforted me during every tear-filled night. You know the struggle it took for me to get to this current state of peace and contentment that yes, still wavers but here you continue to stand and help me continue on.

This journey with you, being able to trust you, hasn't been a smooth, upward path but when I look back at where I was, how broken and distraught I was, how mentally and emotionally unstable I was to where you've brought me now, any bumps or stumbles along the way to you is worth it. I didn't expect to see life past 2014 and here we are. Look at where you brought me. You did this.

I will forever be a work in progress but every day is a new day and opportunity to hit the mark and strive to be better; it's a new opportunity to be who you created me to be. You gave me purpose and it's up to me to recognize it, embrace it and fulfill it with your guidance. Here's to continuing this journey with you.

Contents

Jas Taylor

My Heart Sings to Thee

My heart sings to thee,
Pure, steadfast and true.
You have rescued me,
All praises go to you.

You have brought peace.
Your love restored my soul.
You gathered my heart's brokenness,
And returned it to me whole.

To you I am indebted,
For you have set me free,
And when I'm overwhelmed,
You shield me with your wings.

Gracious is your love.
Sovereign is your name.
You walk with me through life,
Erasing past hurt and shame.

A Psalm Unto You

My heart sings to thee,

Pure, steadfast and true.

You have rescued me,

All praises go to you.

Ode to You (God)

My dearest Lord, thou art my saving grace.
Thou freed my soul from the grasp of Hell.
I'm honored to have thy sun kiss my face.
I long to be near thee; in thee my spirit dwells.
Thine angels guard my being.
It is thy precious cargo they protect.
Every day it is thy glory I am seeing.
Glorious is my God, in thee I shall find rest.
How majestic thou art, my God.
How gracious thou art, my God.

My dearest Lord, how beautiful is thy name.
It brings joy to my ears.
It is as sweet as a comb of honey in the Plains.
I feel comforted when thy presence is near.
Thou rescued me from myself.
Death can no longer reign.
Thou art unwavering when I need help.
My old being is crucified, in thee a new life is made.
How loving thou art, my God.
How magnificent thou art, my God.

A Psalm Unto You

My dearest Lord, how vast is thy pure love.

An overflow of thine agape love fills me.

My eyes are fixated on thy glory above.

Thy name shall keep me in a constant state of glee.

My spirit rejoices at the thought of thee.

A safe haven thou art, my Lord.

I shall eagerly serve thee, basking in thine glory.

I am triumphant in thee; thy word is my sword.

How sovereign thou art, my God.

How cherished thou art, my God.

My dearest Lord, how comforting is thy spirit.

Thy love wraps around my soul.

Thou protect me from myself, my mind is continuously wicked.

It is plagued with self-afflicting thoughts; it drags me into a darkened hole.

Self-harm kept me in bondage.

My self-esteem was shot to Hell.

And yet here I stand, to thee I pay homage;

Thou repaired me to start anew, this miracle I must tell.

How patient thou art, my God.

How reliable thou art, my God.

My dearest Lord how needed thou art in this time.

This world weeps for thy spirit.

Peace of mind has plummeted, our cities plagued by crime.

Remind us thy love is infinite.

Show us the beauty that still abides.

We need an outpouring of thy grace.

Wash us clean like an ocean's tide.

My Lord, shield us from evil's fate.

How limitless thou art, my God.

How needed thou art, my God.

A Psalm Unto You

Sitting at Your Feet

My heart grows weary.
I pray for protection.
Where have you gone?

An outcry fills the earth.
A sadness lingers.
Where have you gone?

A deafening silence.
An exhausted land.
My Lord, my Lord,
Where have you gone?

Nations weep.
Do you hear our cry?
My God, I ask for deliverance.
I ask for grace.

I ask for mercy.
My heart grows weary,
But my spirit remains strong.
I cling to you.

You are my shelter.

You shall provide.

It is you to whom I look.

I shall remain at your feet.

A Psalm Unto You

Through Your Eyes

Oh Lord,

How can you love me?

I am nothing of importance;

A mere speck in this life.

Oh Lord,

What can I offer?

My mind is plagued with doubt.

I fail consistently.

I am nothing special.

Oh Lord,

Why do you want me?

I am tainted.

My belief wavers.

I have done nothing deserving of your grace.

Oh Lord,

What do you see in me?

Oh Lord,

My heart yearns for understanding.

Why me?

My God,

Why not me?

For in me God sees His creation;

A vessel He wants to use.

The Lamb's blood covers me in your grace.

My belief shall never cease nor fail me.

My God,

You have cleansed the stains of sin.

You want me for your purpose and glory.

I am set a part.

I cannot fail in you.

My mind is bathed in your spirit.

My God,

I offer my gifts, my heart, my service.

I place my life on the alter before you.

I have purpose in you.

I am of importance because you love me.

I pray to see my life through your eyes.

Glory, Glory

Glory, glory to the highest one,

For you have sent your only son.

Glory, glory to the prince of peace,

For you have made all nations free.

Glory, glory to the highest king,

Praise to you, all nations sing.

Glory, glory to the Lord above;

Provide your grace, bestow us love.

Glory, glory to Emmanuel,

For you have saved us, in you we dwell.

We sing your praises,

We lift your name,

Glory, glory to the Lamb who reigns!

A Servant's Prayer

Pure.

Pure shall my heart remain to you.

Bless my limbs as they reach for you.

A life spent serving you is a life well spent.

Bless my hands as they labor for you.

Cover my steps;

Lead my feet to you.

Cover my mind

To only think of you.

Bless my tongue

To only speak of you.

Prepare my being to help serve you.

Teach my soul to love you.

Mend my heart to return to you.

Mold my life to live for you.

Here I shall stand and remain for you.

A Psalm Unto You

I will sing praises to the God of my forefathers!
To the God of Esther and Ruth.
To the God of Isaac and Jacob.
Through your word, I will find truth.

I will sing praises to the God of my great grandmother!
Who trusted you with her life.
Who praised you for bringing her over,
And keeping her spirit light.

I will sing praises to the God of my grandmothers!
Who sang hymns in time of need.
Who stretched their hands in worship,
And prayed you'd watch over their seeds.

I will sing praises to the God of my grandfathers!
Who sought you for the way.
Who humbled themselves before you,
And led their families to seek your face.

I will sing praises to the God of my mother!
Who trusted you in the dark.
Who stood through all her tears,
And still gave you her heart.

Jas Taylor

I will sing praises to the God of my fathers!
Who aren't perfect but trust you to renew.
And with their scars from life,
Find grace and healing in you.

I will sing praises to the God who saved me!
Who I had to know for myself.
If you have brought me this far,
I don't need anything else.

Blessed Be the Name of the Lord

Depression haunts me.

The shadow softly knocks at my door.

It follows me.

Grief patiently waits her turn.

Anger is not far behind.

Loss.

Happiness left me.

I call for her, she does not come.

She has not returned.

She does not want to be found.

Life's shackles bind me.

She is bitter.

She encloses her claws around me,

For in her eyes, I am nothing more than

A mere mortal she will defeat

As she tightens her grip.

The earth is suffocated by darkness.

My mind has succumbed to life's turmoil.

Life's sweetness has turned her back on me.

She leaves a sour taste in my mouth.

My God,

I ask for the faith of your servant Job.

Baptize me in your comforting spirit.

My swelled eyes through the tears,

Shall stay focused on your glory.

I shall not be overcome by fleshly sorrows.

For whatever comes my way, you still reign.

For whatever comes my way, you are still sovereign.

For whatever comes my way, you are still God.

For whatever comes my way, blessed be the name of the Lord.

Reference Scripture: Job 1:21

A Psalm Unto You

My Soul Finds Rest in You

I am worn.
24 hours and yet time is still fleeting.
I always find myself whistling while working,
Working away as the clock hands spin.

My body feels the strain of a good ol' day's labor.
My mind refuses to clock out.
These ol' frail bones shall one day return
To the earth you molded it from.

These ol' hands continue to work away.
This ol' mind never ceases to tap out.
This world drains my spirit,
Yet I feel full and replenished.

My soul drinks from your everlasting
Fountain of life to keep it going.
These ol' frail bones shall one day return
To the earth you molded it from,
But my spirit shall live on.

It shall live on long after these ol' frail bones
Return to the soil.
My body aches but my soul is light.

I shall remain satisfied in you.

This world drains my spirit,

But my soul finds rest in you.

A Psalm Unto You

Marathon

Running to you.
I shall run until my legs tire.
I shall jog and never faint.
I pace myself on this journey,
This journey back to you.

Running to you.
I shall walk until my feet swell.
I shall breathe through the hard times.
I pace myself on this journey,
This journey back to you.

Running to you.
I shall crawl until I reach you.
I shall seek you until you're found.
I pace myself on this journey,
This journey back to you.

Home.

I've never been comfortable in unfamiliar spaces.

That never came natural for me.

I've never found comfort in unfamiliar faces.

It takes time for the uneasiness to cease.

I always feel out of place,

A bit left of center if you will.

And yet with your love and grace,

The uneasiness becomes still.

A tranquil escape from noise,

A safe haven I can call my own.

A peaceful retreat in your glory.

I'm grateful to call you my home.

A Psalm Unto You

Palm Sunday

We honor you
Our savior has come
Bless your Holy name!
Sacred is thee
Our battles are won
Bless your Holy name!

My soul is replenished
My spirit sings
Bless your Holy name!
I kneel before you
We celebrate thee
Bless your Holy name!

We honor you
Our savior has come
Bless your Holy name!
You brought us over
You've made man free
Bless your Holy name!

Jas Taylor

Jas Taylor always found comfort through pen and paper. As Taylor spent hours filling spirals, diaries and memo pads with fictional tales, poems and thoughts, the imaginative, inner world became a safe haven and continues to serve as a therapeutic form of self-expression for Taylor. Graduating from Missouri Western State University, Taylor studied journalism at the institution and published her first fiction piece through an online writing contest.

Other work by Jas Taylor include other poetry works releasing in 2021 and lifestyle blog *Modest Petals* found at the website handle www.modestpetals.com. Taylor also plans to release a children's book and prayerfully, a few novels in the near future.

The following pages are entirely for you. Feel free to journal, write down prayers, thoughts, use it as a space to house your doodles or even your own poems. Use the pages as you see fit.

Thank you for taking the time to read the words on the previous pages.

Jas Taylor

Philippians 4:13

A Psalm Unto You

Deuteronomy 31:6

Jas Taylor

A Psalm Unto You

Jas Taylor

Ephesians 6:10

A Psalm Unto You

Jas Taylor

2 Timothy 1:7

www.ingramcontent.com/pod-product-compliance
Lightning Source LLC
Chambersburg PA
CBHW020447030426
42337CB00014B/1436